JASON PIPER

BACK TO SUBURBIA

Reincarnated in Suburban Chicago

iUniverse, Inc.
New York   Bloomington

iUniverse books may be ordered through booksellers or by contacting:

iUniverse
1663 Liberty Drive
Bloomington, IN 47403
www.iuniverse.com
1-800-Authors (1-800-288-4677)

Because of the dynamic nature of the Internet, any Web addresses or links
contained in this book may have changed since publication and may no longer be
valid. The views expressed in this work are solely those of the author and do not
necessarily reflect the views of the publisher, and the publisher hereby disclaims
any responsibility for them.

ISBN: 978-1-4502-6467-9 (sc)
ISBN: 978-1-4502-6468-6 (ebook)

Printed in the United States of America

iUniverse rev. date: 10/01/2010

INTRODUCTION

Back to Suburbia is the true story of Jason Piper, a Chicago area musician and spiritual advisor, who was born with the consciousness of an adult, including memories of previous lifetimes. Also chronicled are some of his near death experiences, and what he brought back from beyond. The ending will have you searching through your own mind to uncover your true self.

FOREWORD

Jason is an extraordinary man who has been born with psychic gifts and has an amazing story to tell. From my own personal experiences as a psychic medium dealing with psychic phenomena, I have had no difficulty relating to Jason's book and trust that you too will find it as exciting and riveting as I did, unable to put it down until finished.

Where Jason differs from other people including most psychics is that he has regained a full recollection of his last previous life and with astonishing clarity can recall dying, then some twenty six timeless years after his death, can remember being born again.

He relates many of his own personal supernatural experiences to us with real examples and demonstrates that in certain situations it is possible to see those in spirit and to communicate with them freely. He also describes in amazing detail two separate occasions of how after praying for help, angels interceded with divine intervention, saving his life.

He introduces us to another dimension of our existence buried in the dark recesses of our subconscious minds that we are usually too busy to connect with or find too difficult to relate to and that is, we existed before birth; exist now in the moment, still exist after death in spirit and are able to reincarnate in the future.

There is a gradual worldwide spiritual awakening to the concept that there is an afterlife in another dimension and Jason advocates that our soul does survive after death in spirit. After all, if we can accept that the living God is Spirit and we are made in his image, then we should be able to accept and reconcile to the growing evidence that we all survive death and live on in spirit.

Therefore, if you have tragically lost a loved one or have a keen interest in spiritual matters, you will find Back to Suburbia both enlightening and comforting.

Lee Anthony Looby, Btheol,
Author of Interviewing Guardian Angels

CHAPTER 1

The End, Or So I Thought...

The very first thing I remember is lying in a hospital bed, writing page after page. It was a darkened room with no view outside. There were windows to the right side of my bed, but I could only see out into the hallway. The smell of pipe smoke and antiseptic permeated the air.

Every so often a nurse would come in and check on me. I was having difficulty breathing but couldn't stop writing. The same feeling of urgency I had to write my last wishes is still with me today. Lots of people, mostly doctors and nurses, some students too, would come to the window and study me. I specifically recall the head doctor. He was a tall, bearded man who always smoked a huge Sherlock style pipe. I hardly noticed, but at times I'd have to put down the pen to rest my hand, that's when I'd see them studying me.

I knew I was quite sick. I had heart trouble before, but it was a cancerous growth in my lung that got me. Cancer was not even remotely treatable back then. Regardless, I kept writing page after page, but eventually I started to weaken. I felt like a circus sideshow. Every time people would stop by and look in at me, I knew they were talking about me. I could also tell the doctors were baffled.

The time soon came when I was too weak to write. While laying there dying, I knew my time had come. While examining my life, I suddenly found myself standing to the left of my bed. I was looking at my own inanimate body from the side.

It didn't take long for me to realize that I had just died. It was such a strange feeling to look at myself from another's perspective. No one could hear me as I tried feverishly to communicate with the staff. I even remember thinking that I was having an out of body experience, that is, until they came in and covered me with a white sheet, a tell-tale sign that someone has died.

As I stood there totally stunned, I realized I was not alone. Someone was there with me, presumably to help me through the death process. I didn't see anyone but I knew they were there because I felt their presence. After the hospital staff covered me up, I was drawn to the side of the room.

The entity and I stepped right through the wall and into a bright, hazy atmosphere. There was a huge mirror that showed me my own life. There was a soothing hum or a vibration sound that engulfed this place. I saw images being played before me on this mirror but it was more like my soul was evaluating its own life.

It seemed like the entity was helping me to evaluate my life as well, moment by moment. I saw both good and bad times. The whole process seemed to fly by really fast. Time didn't appear to be a factor in this realm. Next, I awoke shrouded by fog. Now there were two more faceless, glowing entities, for a total of three. Once again I felt as though I was being evaluated. I saw many mistakes that I made, but was also shown the positive things I did.

Throughout this whole process I didn't say a word; I just observed. The entities never spoke a word to me either, it was all telepathic. It was pretty much self-explanatory; they just allowed me to view my life from my soul's perspective. I couldn't believe some of the stupid choices I had made. I knew I'd definitely do some things differently if I had another chance. I did feel, however, that since I came to this conclusion, I must have learned from my mistakes, thus evolving as a person.

Next, I seemed to be sleeping, or possibly just resting after this ordeal. It seemed to be a period of reflection; I was just lying there meditating, pondering the life I had just lived. I had no idea if 20 minutes or 20 years had just passed. It didn't seem to matter. The next thing I knew I was in a warm, safe place. No one was there, but I could hear voices. It was still very bright. A loud, yet soothing, medium-paced rhythm filled this space.

Primarily, I heard a woman's voice. As time passed, I heard many more voices. As I lay suspended within this environment, I could still remember what happened and the other places from before. It was at this time that I was given the name Jason by one of the entities. I kept repeating it over and over.

At some point I heard her say the name too. I felt like maybe she heard me. It felt great! I was thrilled to think that I was finally having some sort of contact with someone again. Suddenly, the voices got louder. As the voices got louder, the light got brighter.

All of a sudden there was a tremendous amount of light and very loud voices. There were also a lot of familiar sounds and the distinct smell of antiseptic or alcohol, just like the other place. As I looked around, I felt as though I already knew one of these people.

It felt good to finally see the lady whose voice I heard the most. It's a strange feeling to hear someone's voice for a long period of time without having a face to put with it. Now I can see her, she is beautiful, she's my mom. She has big blue eyes and she looks like an angel.

There were a couple of older ladies there too. They were the nurses. They seemed a bit mean. I didn't care for the nurses because they took me away. They always brought me back, but I didn't want to be away from my mom. It was upsetting because I had to stay in the hospital for a few days, but I had to be in the nursery with all the other newborns; I couldn't stay in my mom's room.

One day as the nurse held me, I had a group of people around me taking my picture. I guess I was the cutest baby at Central Dupage Hospital at the time, so they put me on the cover of the Dupage Press. I was supposed to be here on December 24th but I arrived a few days early.

Mayor Views Past, Fut

A progressive independent newspaper published every Thursday and Saturday
By the Press Publications, 173 S. York Rd., Elmhurst, Ill. 60126

20 Cents

HAPPY NEW YEAR!

The DuPage Press

Chapter 2

Home Sweet Home

Finally we were able to leave that place. I hated the smell, and it reminded me of the other place, from before. I remember the exact moment we walked outside and I took my first breath of fresh, outside air. The snow fell very lightly as we walked across the parking lot.

As we drove home I looked up and stared at the streetlights glowing above. It looked like they had halos, like the beings, or entities from before. It was so relaxing to look up at the lights while we cruised down the road snuggled in my mom's arms.

The next days and weeks seemed to fly by. That's when I first remembered my Dad, other than from the hospital. He was nice, but I was aware that I knew him from before.

He looked very familiar to me, I was sure I remembered him from before. Another person was there as well. I got a bad vibe from him and knew instantly that he didn't like me. He was my brother, Joel. He was awesome most of the time, but at first he hated me. He was very jealous of having a new baby around.

One day I was at home with Joel and my mom. Mom left the room briefly so it was just Joel and I. The second Mom left the room Joel jumped up and came over to my bassinet. He covered my face and tried to suffocate me with my blanket. The look on his face was that of murderous intent. She returned just in the nick of time and he stopped. I don't remember much more about that time other than always being with my mom and Joel. My dad was gone a lot.

I was constantly wondering why Joel hated me so much for no apparent reason until I learned that he was supposed to be an only child. He even told my mom that. He obviously didn't take too kindly to the idea of having a baby brother. The weird thing was that sometimes he was totally nice to me. This roller coaster behavior continued for nearly two decades.

As I look back, I have many fond memories of Joel, unfortunately, not as many as the bad ones. My parents were oblivious to these abuses, through no fault of their own. He was a genius and could easily manipulate them. It was either a really good day with Joel, or a really bad day. We did have a lot of fun together and I want to stress that it wasn't his fault that he was feeling that way. It's a good part of the reason that I'm writing this, to help young people in similar situations.

Chapter 3

Artistic Messages

As I got a little older, the majority of my time was spent drawing. It was a way for me to vent my frustrations and to explore my consciousness. It was also a way for me to communicate with others. Mom had headphones on for work so I felt somewhat isolated. I only had my thoughts to ponder.

My mom was a typist, working from home. While she worked, I would usually draw. This is around the time I got my first pet, a Venus flytrap. When I finished my drawings, I would pop up from under her desk and play mailman with a "special delivery." Little did she know, I was trying to deliver very important, precognitive messages.

Even though I find it hard to believe that no one found my morbid artwork disturbing, I also see how getting too busy with the distractions we face in life can make us miss what's really happening. After all, kids, jobs, bills, pets, etc., can drive you crazy!

Most, if not all of my drawings had one consistency, death. Many were random things, like Mammy's heart attack. A lot of them were murders. Most of these drawings did in fact turn out to be precognitive in nature. Copies of a few of the original drawings have been included so you can see them for yourself. Pay attention to your kids folks, they're trying to communicate with you via their artwork. Some things are easier drawn than spoken.

This was also around this time that I had two brushes with death. My mom and I were at a shoe store on Main Street. While she was checking out, I stuck her car keys into the electrical outlet and got shocked right off of my feet. It was a violent jolt of electricity and I was briefly out of my body, watching from the side.

For some reason they had the outlet right on the floor, a very dangerous place to put an electrical outlet. I didn't go to the hospital but my mom and the girl at the cash register were really freaked out. I also remember it made me pee in my pants. I wonder if that jolt activated some of my precognition or other paranormal activity.

Also around this time, my mom and I were driving around doing some errands when we had a terrible accident. As we made a fast left hand turn onto Main Street, my door flew open and my body propelled toward the open door. My mom let go of the wheel and grabbed my left arm at the last second, but my legs were hanging out of the car and got smashed into the sharp metal street sign. We bounced up the curb and smashed into the wall of the church.

It was weird because my mom's brother, my uncle Gary, was sitting right there in his Trans-Am watching the whole thing happen. My mom and I both got nasty gashes and injuries to our legs. She got a really bad slice up her leg that required stitches. It was pretty scary, probably for the people inside of the church too.

I guess that's why these days they make people use car seats for their little ones and builders don't put electrical sockets on the floor anymore. Thank God for these changes, thereby reducing injuries and saving lives.

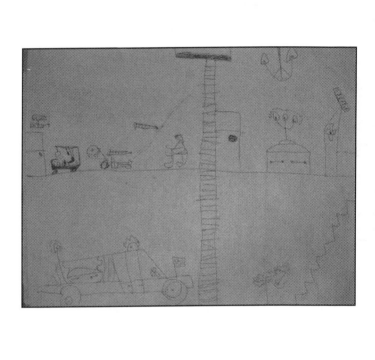

CHAPTER 4

Reliving a War

Oh, by the way, Joel loved to draw too. Unfortunately, he only drew war-themed drawings; most of them focused on World War II, Hitler, and death camps. Those were usually the themes he focused on. Joel was totally obsessed with World War II from a very early age. In junior high he won national recognition for an amazing report he wrote on Hitler and Nazi Germany. He was an amazing student and got straight A's throughout his education.

The times I spent alone with my brother were interesting to say the least. When our parents were around, he was really nice to me, but when they'd leave, he'd flip like a light switch and turn into Hitler, literally.

One day was particularly rough; I remember it clearly. My dad exited the house and left me alone with Joel. Shortly thereafter, two of his friends came over. Joel always wanted to play war and was always a Nazi. Dressed in actual Nazi uniforms from World War II, which were located in a trunk in the attic, he barked orders at his friends to dig foxholes.

Yes, they actually dug numerous foxholes with authentic army shovels all along the Roosevelt Road side of our property. After digging these holes, his friends were ordered to seize the prisoner. Three guesses as to who that was.

Just my luck, I got to be the prisoner in Joel's concentration camp. Oh but this day was just getting started, and got much worse. After a simulated battle, I was captured and beaten by the "Nazis."

It was clear to me that he wasn't playing war, he was re-living one. The look on his face was always dead serious when we'd play war. By then I was used to random, unprovoked beatings but this day was different entirely. This was the first time I actually felt like a tortured prisoner. Next, I was handcuffed and tied up outside to the shed at the far back of our property.

It was a very hot day, downright sultry to be exact. As I stood there handcuffed, I was informed that I would stay there all day in the scorching sun with nothing to eat or drink, while he and his friends went to downtown Wheaton. He said they were going to see a movie and going to the Popcorn Shop, the bike store, to all of my favorite places.

They were gone for hours. They just left me in the raging, midday sun, handcuffed. While cuffed to the shed in the blazing sun, all I could do was pray. I also pondered how this could happen to me. I don't know which was worse, the physical torture from the heat and the sun, or the psychological torture of not being able to go to all of my favorite places with them.

This is part of the reason why I love the cold weather so much. Everyone has always thought that I was nuts because I can wear shorts in 20 degree weather. The reason I do that is because I have been subjected to unspeakable amounts of sun and heat. I get somewhat agitated when I experience extreme heat because it takes me right back to that day, and others like it.

At least when it's cold out you can adjust to it by dressing warmly. It's not possible to do that when it's hot, unless of course you stay in the air conditioning the whole time. Although the air conditioning feels great, it's just not a good existence if you're stuck inside all day.

Aside from the fact that I was hot, tired, and scared, not to mention sunburned to the point of blisters, I was most saddened by the fact that my brother hated me so much. I was confused as to how and or why my suffering brought him such joy. I also could tell his friends felt bad for me but no one ever did anything to stop it. I won't mention any names but they know who they are.

Well, lucky for me that my dad finally came home. It was a close call for Joel because my dad got home just after they returned from downtown Wheaton and took off the handcuffs.

Oh, it would have been a bad day for Joel if he had been caught by my dad. He would've beaten Joel all the way up and back down our street if he had known what was going on when he was gone. After this very close call, Joel became even more careful and calculated. Well, on to some good memories. One of my favorite things to do was to go down to visit my grandparents, Mammy and Pappy, at their house off of President Street.

Chapter 5

My Second Home

I spent tons of time there at 825 Wakeman. I learned countless things from them, and have nothing but the fondest memories of my time here on Earth with them. Mam and Pap's house was also the place where my mom's side of the family would gather for parties and family events. It was great because I'd get to see all of my aunts and uncles, and I'd get to play with all of my cousins who I didn't get to see that often. Ah, ghost in the graveyard was so much fun. I miss them so much!

Mammy was like my second mom. Pappy was my teacher. He taught me everything from gardening, to recycling, to lawn mower maintenance. I would play tricks on Pappy repeatedly. One day he made me really mad, so I made a sign that read "No crappy-Pappy's allowed" and I stuck it on the rec room door. He was less than amused.

By 5 years old, I was tending to a strawberry patch, a huge veggie garden, and a compost heap, and that was just at their house. He's my Pappy and I love him. I feel him with me often. Mammy and I were close like my mom and I are. We're as close as ever and always will be. We are forever fused at the soul and can never be separated. Love is the bond that keeps us all with the ones we love the most, for eternity.

It's important to realize that whether our loved ones are in the physical realm, in between lives, or reincarnated in a different location, our souls are constantly interacting with each other. Once in awhile we have a dream about a deceased loved one and it seems so real, because it is. It's difficult because our conscious minds bleed into the unconscious sometimes and it makes it hard to decipher what is real and what's not.

Needless to say, it was the good times and my connection to the other side that kept me going through the tough times. It was comforting to have most of our family in close proximity; most of them lived in the Wheaton area.

Another one of my favorite people in the whole world is my Aunt Christmas. She lived on a wooded estate adjacent to Cantigny in Wheaton. She was an amazing artist and has had some of her paintings hanging in some prestigious places. One hung in the Mercantile Exchange and still might be there. I, myself, am lucky enough to possess two of her most beautiful paintings, which hang on my wall presently.

She's the one who got me started with art in the first place. Every birthday and Christmas she would stoke me out with the finest of art supplies from Carlson's, and some sweet clothes from Gaede's. I still have the last set of Marvy markers she ever gave me. I definitely remembered her from before too. I just couldn't put my finger on it.

Every Halloween we would go to her home. It was so fun. Aunt Christmas and Uncle Larry would dress up and put on a show for us. She would be a witch and he would be Frankenstein. My favorite scary experience over there was this wire cage they had with a bunch of rubber bats in it that only came out on Halloween. I thought for sure they were real for a long time. Everyone in the neighborhood thought she was a real witch; sorry, she was not. She was very convincing though around Halloween time.

Another one of my favorite, actually THE favorite hobby of mine in this entire lifetime, was going to garage sales with my mom. Resale shops were also on our list of stops. We would go around and use our skills to find jewelry, antiques, and all sorts of treasures.

One of my very first garage sales sticks out a lot because it was one of the first times I ever experienced deja-vu. It was at a sale in Wheaton in a gymnasium adjacent to an old church. I absolutely knew I had been there before. I had flashbacks of myself participating in church services of some sort in a far away time.

Another one of my first garage sales proved to be tragic. We were just off Washington Street in Wheaton. I was about four years old. As we left this particular sale, I noticed a box full of black kittens for free. They were very cute, and I wanted one so badly, but since we had a husky, Shiloh, we couldn't get one because she would eat it.

Well I said screw it and took one anyway. In one quick move I shoved it down my pants and got into the car and we drove away. As we drove, my mom heard meowing coming from under my seat and busted me. By the time we got home she found the kitten.

My dad was so pissed off, but I didn't care. I called him Blackie. The first day went by all right until night fell. Sometime overnight Shiloh got a hold of Blackie and ate him. I was devastated. It was the first time I experienced the death of something I loved and it hurt really badly. Little did I know that it was just the beginning of my bewildering relationship with physical death.

Chapter 6

Valuable Lessons

As school approached, I was both nervous and curious. I was especially happy to get away from Joel, even though he went to the same school that I was about to start attending. He was a really cool brother at school and he always protected me if I needed it.

Well, it was off to kindergarten at Lincoln school. I was so nervous and didn't want to go. After the first day I saw it wasn't that bad. Actually, it was pretty fun. I was in the afternoon class. Thanks, Mrs. Ettel! Right off the bat I knew I was different than the other kids.

One of my very first friends was a little boy named Petey. He was mentally challenged. Everyone used to pick on him, especially this little fat kid named Sebastian. He would just walk up to Petey and push him down or hit him. Petey was a sweet boy who never bothered anyone. He just wanted to play with his trains. He always brought electric trains from home to play with. He was actually a total genius. He would construct amazing structures out of Lincoln Logs and Tinker Toys at a skill level far beyond the Kindergarten level. I will never forget some of the things he built. Petey was, and will always be my friend.

On the second or third day of Kindergarten, Mammy picked me up from school and I told her about Sebastard. She thought I was saying "bastard" and got all ticked off at me. I was actually trying to say Sebastian but all I could say was Sabastard. I really thought that was his name and it turned out to be the perfect nickname.

Another day I saw Sabastard picking on another boy. He was a little blonde kid with a big lion on his backpack. Sabastard was much larger than everyone else and he picked on whomever he felt like. So I stepped in and knocked Sabastard to the ground and he ran away crying. It seemed his bullying days were over, for now. I thought I heard someone call the blonde kid "lion." Since his backpack had one on it, I thought that was his name. I continued to call the kid "lion" for a few weeks until I finally learned his name was Ryan.

By first grade I was having really profound thoughts. I started to poke and prod the other kids to see what they knew, and especially if they remembered being born. It didn't take long for me to come to the conclusion that no one even came close to remembering being born, like I did.

I couldn't comprehend this. How in the world could every single person forget something in just six short years that I remembered like it was a week before? I really thought they were joking, which apparently they were not.

Not far into first grade my family, and teacher, got a big surprise. I was in deep meditation and didn't hear my moody teacher calling me. She thought I was just being insolent and not answering her. She went berserk and screamed at me, so I lashed out with a string of expletives and was suspended from school, in first grade, for 3 days. It was the youngest suspension they ever had.

So here I was with a desk right in the principal's office for three days. I have no doubt in my mind that it was meant to be and here's why. I believe it was on the second day of my suspension, a terrible tragedy unfolded.

Chapter 7

Losing a Friend

My brother's friend, Joe, was killed by a drunk driver while riding his bike. He was riding a silver Hutch Pro Star BMX bike. As I sat there shocked, the secretary pinned a manila envelope on the wall right next to me.

Word for word it said, "We are collecting for flowers for Joe Wiley's funeral."

The first time I read it I couldn't believe it. I actually knew this guy. He lived just a matter of four or five houses down the street from Lincoln School. All day I just read it over and over. I couldn't help but wonder what and where Joe was now. I mean, he surely wasn't "dead." Just his body was. I was fascinated with the concept of death. Joe was also the very first human being I knew who had died.

The next night, my mom, brother, and I went to Hanerhoff funeral home on Main Street in Wheaton. It was the same intersection where I fell out of the car and we crashed into the church. As we walked in the front door, I immediately veered off to the left and went straight to Joe's casket. Mom and Joel went straight over to the family who were seated to the immediate left once inside the actual parlor.

As I approached the casket, I was confused by the sight of a young man pacing back and forth between the casket and the family. When I reached his casket I just stood right there and stared at his face, wondering how this kid, that I knew, was dead. I was also confused by the fact that the guy pacing back and forth looked exactly like Joe.

I knew he had a brother and wondered if it was his twin.

He was wearing a flowery, seventies-style, silk shirt with a maroon, velvet vest over it. He had on a silver skull and crossbones necklace, and his casket was adorned with various BMX magazines. We were all obsessed with our BMX bikes.

So I went over to the family. There was a little boy named Pat sitting on the floor. He was coloring in a dinosaur coloring book. My mom told me that he was Joe's little brother and that they were the only two kids that the Wiley's had.

"Ok, well, who was the guy over there pacing around that looks exactly like Joe?" I thought. It became very clear to me that I was seeing Joe in two places at once, and I wondered if anybody else could see him. Looking back, I fully understand his frustration of not being able to communicate with the living; it is very frustrating.

Interestingly, I actually had a brief encounter with Joe's soul when he looked right at me and noticed that I could see him. Somehow he knew that I was the only person who could see him. I think he noticed me watching him pace back and forth just prior to this brief acknowledgment. I thought he was going to say something to me, but he didn't. He just looked me dead in the eye, and that was it. It was just a brief, very ominous acknowledgment of each other.

Well, Joe's passing fueled my thoughts even further. By second grade I was studying the other kids like a psychiatrist. The classroom was like my office. One day in second grade, while cutting caps inside of my desk, I paused and acknowledged the fact that I had absolutely remembered dying and being reborn in a new body, and everything I ever did up until that point, and no one else seemed to have these memories. That was really, really weird.

The feeling I had was pure isolation. It's really lonely to discover by second grade that you are quite different from the other children. I was OK with it, but felt isolated in some ways at the same time. I was able to acknowledge that it might be to my advantage to be different. So I looked at the bright side of it and kept digging. I was just searching for the answers that I had about life, death, and consciousness.

The next few years were somewhat uneventful, just typical kid stuff. School was both a huge annoyance and a necessity at the same time. Ever since the incident in first grade, I earned the reputation of being a bad kid at school, even though I wasn't. That is until I got sick of the harassment and actually started acting bad.

It wasn't until fifth grade that I learned a valuable lesson. It was a big surprise for me. Even though I got decent grades, I was a tad on the wild side. It was a parent-teacher conference night and I skillfully drafted my mom into the position. She was much more forgiving than my dad, so I always begged her to go, expecting the worst.

I was both shocked and pleasantly surprised when my mom came home thrilled because my teacher, Mr. Declute, was raving about me. At first I thought the raving was bad until I found out it was actually good.

It turned out that Mr. D., unlike most of my previous teachers, was smart enough to see through my shenanigans. He saw, and focused, on all of my good points instead of just talking about my bad ones. He raved about my positive qualities but still pointed out, in a nice way, what I needed to work on.

This taught me that someone had faith in me, a first for me with any other teacher. It also showed me that not only was I lucky enough to have a phenomenal educator, but also a good friend as well. I should also mention that he was Joel's favorite teacher too. This was the boost of confidence I needed to launch me into middle school.

Well, this was also around the time I transitioned from a snare drum to a full-blown drum set. It was a 1967 blue sparkle Ludwig kit with all Zildjian Constantinople cymbals. Drumming has been a passion of mine since birth and it was awesome to finally have a set! Thanks a lot, Greg! He was the guy my dad bought them from. I play my drums for hours every day when I can; I love it!

As sixth grade came and went, I was up to my typical, sometimes quite dangerous, mischievous activity. At the end of seventh grade, I was dealt another terrible blow. My friend, and fellow Cub Scout, Brian, passed away while playing baseball. I believe a heart defect was the culprit. What a shame, such a talented young boy dying from sudden cardiac death.

Ever since Brian's death, I've visited his grave religiously. It's been twenty two years since he died. He's buried just about fifty yards or so from my family plot. He's also buried right by the Wiley's graves. As eighth grade rapidly approached, little did I know, I too, was about to come face to face with death.

CHAPTER 8

Off To Oahu

It was early August 1988. The limousine pulled into our driveway to take us to O'Hare Airport. My mom and I were on our way to beautiful Hawaii.

It wasn't my first time going there. By seventh grade I was already a world traveler having surfed and scuba dived in Hawaii, Puerto Rico, St. Thomas, and even traveled all over France and Germany. I loved all of the sights, especially Le tour d'Eiffel, the Louvre, and Frankenstein's castle, just to name a few.

As we hopped onto the plane, we expected a wonderful trip. It almost ended in a bloody nightmare. It was the second day of our trip, 8-8-88. My Mom was up at our hotel room at the Sheraton Waikiki, while I scampered around looking for something fun to do. I woke up early and decided to go hit the waves.

She said that when she gets up that she'll be going to the pool. She wouldn't go into the ocean anymore; she's deathly afraid of sharks. My dad used to make her dive in all sorts of sketchy places and she was scared. I'm sure she'll never step into the ocean ever again.

It was about 10:00 A.M. on Waikiki beach. I raced out into the water to snorkel around by myself. I bumped into a local Hawaiian kid who informed me of a sale down the street at the surf shop. That was all I needed to hear and I was racing up to the hotel to beg my mom for the money. Since she IS the best Mom in the world, she obviously gave me the money to go get a boogey board, and that's exactly what I did.

Within minutes my new friend and I were paddling out to find some waves. Waikiki is not a very popular surf spot. The killer waves are on the North shore at Bonzai Pipeline or Sunset Beach. He said if we paddle down near Diamond Head there would be sets of 4 to 6 foot waves. We found the waves but they were pretty far out there. We just looked for the locals and they brought us right to the waves.

We proceeded to go 100 to 200 yards out from shore. We were so far out that the people on the beach looked like ants. The little boy was scared to be beyond the reef, but I didn't care. I wanted to be way out so I could be the first one on and the first one off the waves. I wanted to get out of there before we encroached into the locals' area; they get really aggravated when you do that.

So on we surfed until we started drifting into their space. Looking back, I see we were totally nuts to be hanging out beyond the reef wall in deep blue sea. The kid was scared to death and wanted to move in closer to shore. He probably knew what I was ignoring: A. sharks feed in the morning and at night, and B. they lurked just beyond the reef wall for prey items. It wasn't that I didn't know these facts; I just didn't care. I caught a nice wave and thought I'd try something I'd never attempted, to stand up on a boogey board.

These boards are much shorter than a typical surfboard. I did manage to stand up and was able to ride out a small wave until I noticed that the guy ahead of me went down hard. I was catching up to him fast but before I could react, the guy's board shot out of the water like a rocket. His board came right down smack dab on my forehead. Imagine a six-foot long, fiberglass surfboard complete with sharp fiberglass slivers sticking up all over it, landing on your face.

Apparently the guy hadn't felt it necessary to secure his ankle leash. That's why surfboards have a leash in the first place, to keep people from getting hurt and to keep your board from getting away from you.

In a flash, I was knocked off of my board and into the water. The huge surfboard had ripped my forehead wide open. Bordering on consciousness, I looked down to find myself in a gigantic blood pool, with no board to hold onto. When I looked over at my little friend, he was as white as a ghost. He just turned around and pretty much walked on water towards shore.

My head was pounding like a bass drum and I was blinded and choked by all of the blood. It was spurting out faster than I could wipe it away. I looked back and realized I was all alone. This was very disappointing to say the least. Here I am floundering in a gigantic blood pool, bordering on consciousness, and no one even helped me out. I was losing consciousness fast and had nothing to keep me afloat. I watched helplessly as my board floated away in the distance.

I knew that if a shark could smell a drop of blood from a mile away, I must have been attracting scores of them. I would have been quite a tasty morsel for them to munch on. This was by far the loneliest, most desolate feeling I had ever felt. I knew that at any second I could be taken by a shark or some other predator. I couldn't stop thinking about my poor mom and how she'd have to identify what, if any, of my remains were left. That's if they were even recovered in the first place.

As I floated on my back to keep myself above water, I just stared up into the beautiful sky and prayed to God. I just flat out asked him (or her) to intervene if they felt it in their heart to do so. I knew that my insolent behavior had once again gotten me into trouble and that I had put myself there, I just wanted one more chance at life. I also promised to make up for everything bad that I had ever done if I was somehow spared.

It was at this exact moment that I was bumped from underneath. It was quite a forceful impact, coming from my left side, hitting my hip and thigh. It was a large shark. I saw his beady eyes looking right at me. It bumped me again and actually lifted me out of the water. I pushed off of his face and felt his sandpapery skin; he felt a lot like the surfboard. I also noticed his brown skin and stripes.

My life started to flash before me like many people report during a near death experience. As the fish receded, I felt arms lift me right out of the water. We started moving at a tremendous rate of speed. I was somehow on my back looking up.

I felt the scratchy, sandpapery feeling on my back and thought I was riding on the sharks back. I didn't know what was happening until I finally wiped off enough blood to see that I was on a board piloted by a tall, faceless, glowing entity. We were going so fast that I'm positive that it wasn't humanly possible. We were going at such a high rate of speed that I actually toyed with the idea that I was already dead and was being surfed into the afterlife. It was so surreal.

The next thing I know is that I'm on the beach being treated by some paramedics. I asked where the person was who saved me, but no one ever was located. I looked down and saw that my board was right there with me even though I watched it float far away from me while I was half-conscious in the blood pool. When you're saving someone from a tiger shark, the last thing you'd ever think to do is go after the person's board; it just wouldn't be a priority. The faceless, glowing entity was nowhere to be found, and was never seen by anyone but myself.

Next, my mom came flying down the beach with the hotel manager. She was so scared because she thought that I had gotten eaten by a shark. We were whisked off to the hospital where I underwent the very long, very painful process of having each grain of sand removed from my face one by one. Then I had to get the deep wound stitched up.

The very next day I was back in the water with my lucky board. Needless to say, I was much more cautious and did not venture beyond the reef wall.

The rest of the trip was spent snorkeling, dining out, and shopping. There was no doubt in my mind that I had just been spared a gruesome death via divine intervention. Believe it or not, angels are everywhere. I knew my life was spared for a reason. I just didn't know what that reason was, yet. I felt a flood of awareness come over me and a new appreciation for my life.

I'd also like to point out that due to the strange date, 8-8-88, I became very interested in numerology. On the last day of our trip, we went to a phone hut. It's just a huge tiki hut filled with payphones to call the mainland. We called Mammy and Pappy and talked for a few minutes. I couldn't put my finger on it, but I had a feeling that I'd never see Mammy ever again. It was just a gut wrenching, sick feeling.

CHAPTER 9

Precognition

When we got home, I tried to tell my friends what had just happened to me. They either didn't understand or didn't care. The rest of August was strange. I spent almost every minute in class staring out of the window in deep meditation. It was about the third week of September when I had a series of daytime premonitions, or precognitive daydreams.

The first one was very straightforward. I was sitting in my math class with Mr. Graphlund during the last period of the day. I was looking out of the window when everything shifted focus. I had a flash of my dog Shiloh's face. As I approached Roosevelt Road I had another flash, this time of the tree in the backyard of our house where we clip him to go potty.

The line was bare and I saw Shiloh was gone. Fifteen minutes later when I got home, I saw the exact picture that flashed in my head. It was my first conscious premonition that I can recall, aside from the drawings from when I was younger.

Lucky for us, we got him back. They had him waiting for us down at the pound. The very next day, I had another vision. I thought it was odd that it was the same exact time of the day, last period. I was gazing out of the window and I had a vision of this creepy, sinister-looking guy pulling up to me in a car and trying to talk to me.

While walking home that day, my friend Jay and I threw some pebbles at a passing car and it screeched to a stop. It was the strange guy from my vision. He rolled down his window and started screaming at us. He said, "You little bastard! I'm a DuPage County judge and I know who you are!" I knew he was full of crap because if he really knew who I was, he'd know that both of my parents work at that very courthouse. It turns out he really was a judge, and still is to this day.

With a flip of my finger and a smile from ear to ear, I was off like the dickens. This goofy behavior was typical for kids that age, well, at least for me and my friends.

Having these visions wasn't all bad; it opened up a whole new world for me to explore, the world of extra sensory perception, or E.S.P. I wondered if my continued consciousness or my massive head injury had something to do with the increased frequency of these events.

I already knew I was definitely reincarnated, but I wasn't sure if that had anything to do with the precognition. I started to have visions more and more frequently, some even while I was asleep.

My dad even took notice. I would fall asleep watching television with him and start talking to him and acting out scenarios in my sleep. When I awoke, he'd grill me about the memories, but I thought he was pulling my leg, I had absolutely no recollection of them. That was really weird.

He even noticed that most of the time when I'd have these memories, my eyes were wide open. That really got me thinking about the subconscious mind as well. I found it amazing that my subconscious mind could accomplish so much with no recollection of it at all while conscious.

Chapter 10.

An Angelic Visit

Once again I got a sick, disturbing feeling. I could sense and smell a tragedy coming by paying close attention to the aroma in the air and the vibratory rate of the energy around me. It might sound strange, but I have all but perfected this skill.

As September came, I felt sicker and sicker. By the end of the month I knew that something awful was going to happen. It was the night of September 29th, 1988, at approximately 10:30 P.M. Central Standard Time.

I had just drifted off to sleep, when suddenly I awoke to find mammy next to my bed, on the right side. I was shocked and I jumped up out of bed. She took my hand

and told me not to be scared. She hugged me and we spun above our house, way up in the sky, around and around.

All of a sudden I was slammed right back down on my bed. I knew it wasn't a dream. I also knew she had died. I felt as though she had given me some sort of information, similar to a download.

I flew out of bed and bolted to my mom's room. I looked in on her and, before I could say a thing, she popped up and looked right at me. I could tell by the look on her face that she also knew. She had that just-got-woken-up-in-the-middle-of-the-night look, times a hundred.

I told my mom we needed to go down to the clubhouse and call Mammy from the payphone. We didn't have a phone during this time period so we used that one. I told my mom about how Mammy just came to me and told me that she had just died. Mom said it was probably just a weird dream. I knew she was wrong and I was totally freaked out. Two people usually don't share the same dream; however, it is possible.

It wasn't even that. When something like this happens to you, you don't just think that it happened, you know it did. So obviously I couldn't sleep and just lay there for hours. Somehow, I finally drifted off.

It seemed as though only a minute had gone by and I was opening my eyes in the sunlight. All I could hear were the faint sounds of crying, sort of muffled. I immediately knew they were there to tell us that Mammy had died. Sure enough, I walked out to the living room and there was my aunt Marcy, my dad and my mom.

They told me that last night, at approximately 11:36 P.M. Eastern Standard Time, Mammy died of a massive heart attack. I was devastated, but not at all surprised. Here was a lesson in itself: always trust your gut feelings. This was proof that last night really did happen. I can't believe my mammy chose me out of all of her loved ones to come and visit in preparation for the news.

Actually, I can totally see why. She was like my second mom. I spent more time with her than anyone else. She babysat me on a daily basis and I even lived there for 3 or 4 years. She used to see my drawings too. I wonder if she saw the one that predicted her own massive heart attack and subsequent death. I drew it at her house and right on her Social Security statement. I'm pretty sure I was trying to tell her so she could prepare or possibly avoid the whole situation.

New payment amount

Starting with the July 2 payment, your Social Security payment is increased by 7.4 percent. This is an automatic increase based on the rise in the cost of living. Your new monthly payment amount is $ 321.00 . Under a change to the law, benefits are now paid only in exact dollars. This means that a payment with extra cents has been rounded to the next lower dollar before being sent to your bank or other financial institution.

If you are paying for Medicare medical insurance, your new monthly premium of $12.00 for the 12-month period beginning July 1, 1982 has already been subtracted in determining the above monthly payment amount.

Change of address

Although your Social Security checks are not sent to your home, we must keep your correct mailing address so we can send you important information about changes in Social Security and changes that may affect the amount of your monthly payment. By law, your financial organization cannot provide us with your present address. Your monthly Social Security payments can be stopped if we cannot locate you to verify your continuing eligibility.

The address shown above is the latest address we have for you. If it is correct, you don't have to do anything.

If the address is not correct, please write your new address above and mail it back to us in the prepaid envelope that is enclosed with this notice. Or, call, write, or visit any Social Security office to give us your new address.

If you plan to move in the future, hold on to the address card and envelope so you can report your new address to us when you do move.

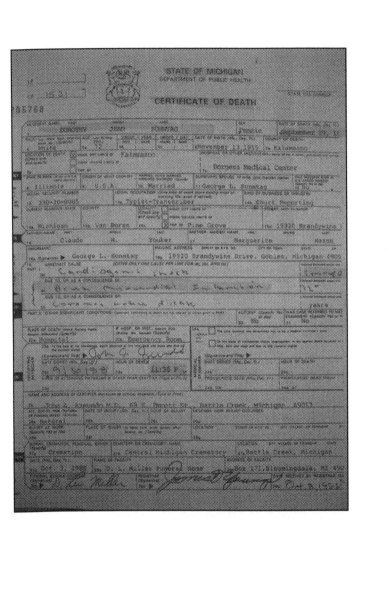

STATE OF MICHIGAN
DEPARTMENT OF PUBLIC HEALTH

CERTIFICATE OF DEATH

905768

DECEDENT NAME: DOROTHY JEAN SONNTAG — SEX: Female — DATE OF DEATH: September 29, 19

RACE: White — AGE: 72 — DATE OF BIRTH: November 11, 1913 — Kalamazoo

PLACE OF DEATH: Kalamazoo — HOSPITAL OR INSTITUTION: Borgess Medical Center

BIRTHPLACE: Illinois — U.S.A. — MARRIED — SURVIVING SPOUSE: George L. Sonntag

SOCIAL SECURITY NUMBER: 330-30-8085 — USUAL OCCUPATION: Typist-Transcriber — KIND OF BUSINESS: Court Reporting

RESIDENCE STATE: Michigan — COUNTY: Van Buren — CITY: Pine Grove — 19320 Brandywine

FATHER NAME: Claude W. Youker — MOTHER MAIDEN NAME: Marguerite Mason

INFORMANT: George L. Sonntag — MAILING ADDRESS: 19320 Brandywine Drive, Gobles, Michigan 4905

PART I
IMMEDIATE CAUSE: Cardiogenic shock
DUE TO: Acute myocardial infarction
DUE TO: Coronary artery disease

PART II OTHER SIGNIFICANT CONDITIONS:
AUTOPSY: No — WAS CASE REFERRED TO EXAMINER: No

PLACE OF DEATH: Hospital — Emergency Room

SIGNATURE: John C. [signature]
DATE SIGNED: 9/30/88 — HOUR OF DEATH: 11:35 P.

NAME AND ADDRESS OF CERTIFIER: B. John A. Azzoudo, M.D., 69 S. Pocost St., Battle Creek, Michigan 49017

MANNER OF DEATH: Natural

BURIAL, CREMATION, REMOVAL: Cremation — CEMETERY OR CREMATORY NAME: Central Michigan Crematory — LOCATION: Battle Creek, Michigan

DATE: Oct 3, 1988 — NAME OF FACILITY: D. L. Miller Funeral Home — ADDRESS: Box 171, Bloomingdale, MI 490

FUNERAL DIRECTOR SIGNATURE: D. Lee Miller — REGISTRAR: James P. Young — DATE RECEIVED BY REGISTRAR: Oct 3, 198

In the following days and weeks, I was very depressed. I was both saddened and amazed by what had happened. Even though I was sad, I felt very comforted at the same time. I knew what so many didn't, that there are absolutely no two ways about it: life continues, even thrives, after physical death. I still felt Mammy very close to me after her "death." I'd even say I felt closer, or even at one with her.

So, I stood tall for mom and Pappy after she died. Maybe that's why Mammy chose me, because she knew I was strong, and maybe even that I knew what to do with all of this information. It was painful seeing my Pappy. He was absolutely destroyed. Luckily, he found another love to keep him happy until he sees his Mammy again in the future.

Anyway, so what if I couldn't see her. I could feel her, which is a much more trusted sense than vision in my opinion. Your eyes can play tricks on you, but what you feel in your heart is what's real. That's why I said earlier, Mammy, mom, and I are together fused at the soul and could never be separated. Our love for each other runs deeper than the deepest depths of the sea. It's immeasurable in Earthly terms.

I still feel her around me often. It's been twenty-one years and I feel her around me stronger than ever. I often wonder if she is an angel, or possibly if she's already back here for another mission. Either way, we will meet again, whether it's in another lifetime, or in-between, or at the end, in Heaven. Either way, there's no doubt in my mind that we will all end up with our truest of loves, together in Heaven.

Well, as time passed I never really got over the loss, simply because I never really lost her. What I did lose was the physical contact of actually seeing her. There are times when I'll be doing something, and I'll feel her presence and stop, then I smell her perfume and I know she's next to me. It's so comforting to know she watches over me.

CHAPTER 11

Signs From Above

Shortly after Mammy's death, another very interesting thing happened. Well, first off, back in 1984 Mam and Pap sold the house at 825 Wakeman and moved to their Michigan house on Lake Brandywine. It was their dream to retire there. Every week since they moved, Mammy would call my mom at her office at the Courthouse in Wheaton to chat.

My mom looked forward to those talks a great deal. She would call at the same time every Friday, like clockwork. A few months had passed and one Friday it was business as usual at the office. Mom was very busy and the phone rang. What she heard caught her so off guard that she almost fainted. It was Mammy on the other end of the line. All she said was; "Mere? Mere?" My mom's name is Meredith. It was definitely Mammy's voice and seemed to have the stereotypical static in the background.

I say stereotypical because I've come to realize that phone calls from disembodied individuals are quite common. I highly recommend reading <u>Phone Calls from the Dead</u> by D. Scott Rogo and Raymond Bayless (1979), a compilation of real cases of phone calls from beyond, and a fabulous, informative read.

Well, this string of communications between Mammy, my mom, and I were far from over. Another tradition they had was that Mammy would send my mom ten dollars every year for her birthday. She'd have to be careful too, because Pappy was incredibly tight with his money and he might have gotten mad at her. This was obviously the first year she wouldn't receive that little present, or would she?

It was my mom's first birthday since Mammy died, and she was really sad. As mom prepared to go out for a jog, she felt Mammy's presence nearby. She began her jog and headed down the path. Halfway through her jog she noticed something unusual down on the ground right in front of her.

It resembled an unusual looking maple leaf. But, upon closer inspection she realized it was actually a ten-dollar bill, perfectly folded origami style, into a Maple leaf. She felt Mammy's love engulf her and she immediately knew it was a sign that she was all right.

People need to realize that we're all spiritual beings, or souls, who operate physical bodies just like we operate cars. Interestingly, cars are very similar to our bodies in the sense that a car will never, ever drive itself, (unless it's Herbie), until we intelligently control, or drive the car.

Our bodies would never move unless they were driven by a soul, or conscious observer. We need to do this in order to sustain ourselves within this physical environment that we call Earth. Even when a car is driven by a person, it has wear and tear, and things eventually break or go wrong with it, just like our bodies. Once a car is beyond repair, we simply go out and get a new one, just as we do when our bodies are beyond repair. Before we can just acquire a new body, we need to relax within the incubative state, as I call it, so our souls can recuperate. It's a time of reflection.

Chapter 12

Tragedy on 64

As high school began, I was headed in no particular direction. I started off playing football and wrestling. It was fun and things started coming together nicely. I met a group of cool people and good friends but out of nowhere, a move to Aurora landed me in a total hellhole. I hated saying goodbye to North and to all of my friends that I met there.

Well, this place was more like a prison than a school. It was so bad in fact that they had to move the police right into the school. These were not rent-a-cops or robo-cops; these were real Aurora police officers.

So, needless to say after a few months I was out of there. There was no way in hell I was about to waste one more second at that place. I said, "see ya" and got a car and a full-time job instead. I went from one pointless, low-end job to another, even juggling two simultaneously. I learned a lot from those jobs, but more importantly, I made some long-term friends.

Even though I was a responsible kid, I felt as though I wasn't living up to my full potential, not even close. Just when things started looking up, tragedy loomed, yet again.

It seemed like a normal day at first. I'm not one hundred percent about the details, but by the end of the day I was informed that two of my good friends, Jeff and Heather, were killed in a horrific automobile accident on North Avenue. There was another boy in the car who survived but I didn't know him too well.

My friends, Jeff and Heather, were mangled in a twisted pile of steel that day, and it broke my heart. Jeff played football with me and was such a kind, funny guy. Heather was a sweet, beautiful girl who had a very bright future.

Hundreds of people attended their wakes. They were so severely injured that Heather had to have a veil draped over her casket to somewhat obscure the view of her face.

Ironically, her casket rested in the exact spot, in the exact parlor, where my brother's friend, Joe Wiley's casket was placed.

I noticed Heather sitting near who I believe were her parents. It was apparent to me that she was trying to console them. I often wonder if anyone else in attendance could see her. Maybe I'll never know, but if anyone did see her there, I'd love to hear from you.

I didn't see Jeff at his wake, only his physical body. Then again, there were hundreds of people there and I was already totally overwhelmed. It would have been hard to decipher between the living and the disembodied since they appear to be pretty similar to each other every time I see them.

For the next few months, I was totally trying to initiate contact with them. I succeeded only twice, both times communicating with Jeff only. Maybe I didn't have a close enough bond with Heather, I'm not sure.

I still visit their graves to this very day. I can only hope to see them in the spiritual realm or possibly in another lifetime. Wherever they are, I'm sure they are fine and have moved on to new adventures. At this point, I felt like the Grim Reaper. It just seemed like death followed me everywhere.

The next few years went by quickly and were somewhat uneventful. I was playing in a couple of bands and working an ultra-boring, low-paying job. The only good thing about it was that I worked by myself and my boss didn't care what I did, as long as I did my job well, which of course I did. Thanks John!

By now it was 1996. I did lots of drumming, reading, thinking, drawing, etc. I worked the night shift so I could read one or more books, depending upon their length, in one night. I burned through hundreds of books for the few years that I worked there. Towards the end of that job, I considered writing this book. I felt like I had finally found a direction, or at least a vision that was positive, which I thought I could achieve.

I was a little bit on the fence about it because I wasn't sure if anyone would want to read about my life story. So I played with the idea of writing an autobiography for about two years until right around Christmas of 1997.

I had never even remotely considered writing a book. It was something that never entered my mind up until that point. Usually writers are doctors or proven authors right?

Not true. Anyone can write a book regardless of education or credentials. I've always said that everyone should write an autobiography and hand it out to the people that they know. How else can we possibly understand each other fully unless we know where and what we've each encountered in our lives?

In order to know someone, we must know what he or she has been through. You don't have to have had any weird experiences to have an interesting story. After all, every single one of us is unique, a one of a kind story within ourselves.

CHAPTER 13

Angels by My Side

One day at the end of January, I was carrying on with my day as usual. There was nothing out of the ordinary to report as I drove around doing my errands. Later that night I was supposed to meet two of my good friends, James and Sean, at Bowling Green in West Chicago. It's a local bowling alley/bar on Roosevelt Road.

I would have gone with them but I had to run up to Hanover Park to see a friend. While visiting with this friend, I decided to call James and tell him that I'd just meet them at Bowling Green.

While I sat there, I became unbearably queasy out of nowhere. It was that very familiar, gut wrenching feeling I'd felt so many times before. It never failed, every time I got that feeling, something terrible would happen shortly thereafter.

I later learned that the stomach is referred to as the second brain. Stress or anxiety can make you very sick and this typically will manifest with an upset stomach. It seemed that somehow over the years my digestive system became incredibly tuned-in to these vibrations around me.

By this time, I was literally shaking. I couldn't put my finger on it but I felt as though I was about to have to deal with a personal tragedy of some sort. It had a somewhat different feel about it entirely.

I could feel a distinct, profound deviation within the energy around me. I had to leave. I hopped into my mom's car and drove south on County Farm Road. Thank God my Mustang went into the shop the day before. If I had been in my car that day, you would not be reading this. It sat really low to the ground and had glass t-tops.

So, I proceeded to turn west onto Army Trail Road. By the time I had reached Route 59, I felt impending doom lurking nearby. It was a stressful feeling knowing that something negative was about to happen to me, but I had no precognitive dream or image to allow me to pin point the location and/or manner of this occurrence. All I could tell was that I knew I was about to be in an accident of some sort. I had no idea where or when; I just knew that it was close.

I cautiously executed a left turn onto Route 59. The feeling grew stronger as I traveled further south. After driving for approximately three minutes, I felt compelled to pull off to the side of the road to essentially let time "pass" me by. I was hoping to avoid the accident by stalling. I made a right-hand turn on a small street right in front of St. Andrew's Golf Course in West Chicago.

My friend, Dennis, lived right there. I was going to stop by and delay a few minutes, but it was a little on the late side so I decided against it. I sat up in my seat and said, "Hey, you're just being paranoid." I reluctantly pulled back onto Route 59 and proceeded south.

I will tell you first-hand, there is nothing more frustrating to me than knowing that something tragic is about to happen and not being able to prevent it. My senses were vibrating at a rate I have yet to experience again to this day. As I accelerated, I could smell the tragedy looming.

As I approached North Avenue, I was shaking and sweating. When I reached the strip mall I noticed a quick flash between the McDonald's and the gas station. It was a set of headlights, and I was now at the intersection of North Avenue and Route 59, one of the deadliest intersections in Illinois.

As I neared the light, I saw the same headlights coming right at me at a very high rate of speed. I looked up at the light because I actually thought that I was about to run the light. I knew the other guy was going much too fast to stop. When I looked up, I had the green light all day long. Bear in mind that I was being extremely cautious and actually expecting this accident at any moment. I wasn't about to blow any red lights.

Suddenly I was in the intersection. I looked to the left and "BAM!" I ate the front end of this guy's car at approximately 60 to 70 miles per hour. In an instant, I was hit with an incredible amount of force right into my body, no seat belt, no airbags, nothing. While I lay battered, in and out of consciousness, I remember this nice lady talking to me through the twisted metal. She said she was a nurse and that she saw the whole collision happen. She said she would stay with me and that I'd be all right. I mumbled something to her about my mom, but I can't remember exactly what I said, though I clearly remember the frightened look on her face and her sad looking eyes.

I lost consciousness again and suddenly found myself standing at the northeast corner of 59 and North Avenue looking southwest. I was standing there watching this horrible accident unfold and saw them trying feverishly to extricate some guy from the wreck. It was really weird because I knew that I was just doing something a few minutes before that.

I felt absolutely horrible for the guy. He looked like he was pinned in the car. Once again, I had this nagging feeling that I was supposed to meet someone somewhere, but I couldn't remember who or where. As I started to retrace my steps, I was drawn back to the accident. I couldn't take my eyes off of the scene but I knew I was just doing something a few minutes earlier. I couldn't shake that feeling for the life of me.

Now I started to retrace my steps, moment by moment. All of a sudden, I realized that someone was with me at the street corner. Actually, I had one person to either side of me. It seemed perfectly natural to me that there would be other gawkers that were watching the accident, but I didn't really even acknowledge them at first.

Suddenly the guy was freed from the wreck. He was placed on a stretcher and whisked away towards the ambulance. I'll never forget the way this ambulance looked. It was one of those Mobile Intensive Care units. It was huge and looked like a combination between a fire truck and an ambulance. Another odd characteristic was that it was either neon yellow or lime green. It was quite unusual.

As they ran with the stretcher, I could tell the guy was in serious trouble. I started to retrace my steps once again: I was at Chris' house. I left and started going to meet James and Sean. I was cruising down Route 59. I got that terrible feeling, and then I got hit by that idiot in the car. That's when it got really crazy for me.

On their way to the ambulance, the guy's head flopped over to the side and was facing me. I saw his face, and low and behold, it was me. Everything around me started to spin. I felt the people on either side of me wrap their arms around me, as if to comfort me. I could not believe that the guy on the stretcher was me. I mean, I felt fine. It quickly became clear that I was dead.

As I realized that I was dead, or at the very least, disembodied, I screamed with everything that I had that I would not depart my present life. I found myself pleading with God, yet again, that it was not my time.

I just flat-out refused to leave. I would not go. It was then that I saw their faces. They were so beautiful. It was Jeff and Heather. They were there for me in my time of need, just a few hundred yards from where they themselves had died.

I embraced them, thanked them, and told them I loved them. We stood right near the curb on the northeast corner of the intersection. A foggy veil separating our two realities ran right down the middle of North Avenue running east/west. They appeared to be trying to get me to cross over with them, but I couldn't go. My time here was far from over, God willing.

Once again, I could only think about my mom. Jeff and Heather crossed North Avenue and disappeared into the fog. It wouldn't be the last that I'd see of them.

With an enormous "THUD" I awoke inside of the ambulance, numb from the waist down and vomiting blood profusely. I grabbed the paramedic and pulled him very close and said, "I can't feel my legs."

The next thing I knew, I awoke in the hospital in severe pain. After a few long days my sensation came back.

Then the really severe pain set in. I was so much enjoying still being alive that I didn't even mind being in pain. It's hard to explain, I actually loved the fact that I could still experience pain.

When I got home I was bedridden, I couldn't walk or even take one step. Even though I was saved, yet again, I still had the feeling of impending doom. Now it seemed as though it was focused on someone else entirely.

CHAPTER 14

Losing Joel

As the weeks dragged on, I could not shake this feeling. I once again came to the conclusion that I should never, ever dismiss my feelings as paranoia again. For some reason, I became fixated with my brother, Joel. I couldn't stop thinking about him for three straight days.

I just couldn't stop thinking about him no matter how hard I tried. It was like he was near me, trying to tell me something. My memories of my brother are by no means all bad. We shared many good times when he wasn't having past life memories.

He used to tell everyone that I was a good singer and drummer. He told them how I could sing like a lot of different artists from Geddy Lee of Rush to Phil Collins, to Les Claypool of Primus. He particularly liked my Les Claypool impression. One day my friend, Brian, and I were in a full-on jam of "My Name is Mud" by Primus.

Brian was on the bass and I was playing drums and singing through my headset microphone. Joel stopped by with a couple of friends and they popped their heads in. When they realized we were actually playing the song ourselves, they were amazed. They thought we were just blasting Primus through my stereo. After that we got along much better. Maybe Joel, being the phenomenal musician that he was, and still is, appreciated my musical talents. If anyone could appreciate good music, it was Joel.

It was February 12th, 1998, Lincoln's birthday. I was kicking back with my friend using some medicine that he just brought back from Amsterdam. I was still in severe pain, so the more actual medicine the better. It's good for the mind and the body.

Everything seemed to be all right except the still nagging feeling that something big was about to happen. As we relaxed and enjoyed the medicine, the front door started to knock. It was a loud knock and it startled us. It was definitely more like pounding than knocking and it even started to move around the apartment, first to my bedroom, then around the corner to the patio door.

When I opened the front door, there stood a few policemen and a priest. They were there to inform me that they had just found Joel in a hotel room in Arlington Heights, dead, of an apparent suicide. I was stunned. When I told Mom, she almost dropped dead of a massive heart attack. It was very difficult to have to tell my mother that her oldest child just killed himself, and then see her react to what I had just told her.

I immediately tried to get a hold of my dad, but was unsuccessful. Someone in the family finally broke the news to him. He had treated Joel somewhat bad over the years and was displaying huge amounts of guilt and grief.

Well, now I understood why I was so fixated on my brother. I believe it was him trying to communicate with me and/or prepare me for what was coming. He was well aware of how Mammy came to me, so maybe he followed suit. A few days later I found myself at yet another funeral. This time it was at Kampp's. There were tons of people in attendance.

People filed by his casket all day long and well into the night. I never even considered him taking his own life.

It now seemed as though this may have been why I was spared in the accident just three weeks prior. Maybe God knew my mom would once again need my strength to get through this tremendous loss.

It's crazy to me that my brother and I came within just three weeks of each other both dying. Well, who knows? Maybe if I had died in that crash, it would've given Joel the strength to stand up straight and help our mom through it. Sadly, I doubt it. In actuality, it would've probably just aggravated his depression and/or made him feel even worse for the way he treated me. Once again, I guess we will never know.

I saw my brother attend his own wake. He was there to see first-hand the pain and misery that he had put his loved ones through. I also saw two older ladies and one really old lady sitting there with him, seeming to console him. He had his face buried in his hands as the women tried to make him feel better, to accept it. When I described the appearance of the women to my mom, especially the robust, curly, white-haired lady with a huge pearl necklace and blue and white polka-dot dress, she said it was a dead ringer for one of her older, deceased relatives. I'm pretty sure it was her grandmother.

The next day was the funeral and the burial. As if it wasn't weird enough, as the funeral service started I could not take my eyes off of my grandfather's headstone. I just kept going back and forth between my brother's casket and my grandfather's headstone. It reminded me of all the times we went to the cemetery to our family plot to visit our deceased relatives.

Every time we went there, I'd look at my grandfather's stone and have memories of a time long ago. I'd just lose myself in thought and have memories of myself in old downtown Wheaton. We would visit my dad's father and his mother, Grandma Nan. She was a very sweet lady who loved us dearly, but lived all the way in Tennessee. I rarely ever got to see her and my Grampa Theo. We all owe Theo a great deal, for he was a well-known doctor who helped Dr. Jonas Salk invent the Polio vaccine. Polio was a horrible disease, and if not for their lifetimes of work, it might still be killing people today. Thanks, Grampa Theo!

CHAPTER 15

Soul Searching

I never knew my dad's dad because he died twenty-six years before I was even born. It made it even more unusual that I was having these memories only when I was looking at his headstone.

I had intense memories of being in Wheaton decades before. I was always the same guy, a well dressed, middle-aged man who smoked a lot. I also had memories of traveling abroad and driving from Wheaton to Chicago in a very old car. I believe it was a Model T. As a matter of fact, most of my memories were from my store on Jeweler's Row in Chicago.

When we would leave the cemetery, I would wonder why I was having such vivid memories of myself in a far away time. I was curious as to how I could remember details of someone's life who I had never met before. It made me look closely at my own life to see if I could find some sort of correlation between the two of us.

The more I examined my own life, the more of his life seemed to flood into my consciousness. I started to remember. One day while I was meditating at the cemetery, I felt something click in my brain. It was just like a veil was finally lifted off of my head. I finally did remember. I started to have more and more memories, day and night.

My mom and dad seemed to be adjusting to my brother's death, but it was not easy for them. It was also incredibly hard on my dear Pappy. He was so distraught over Joel's death. When you're eighty years old and you have cancer, the very last thing you expect to happen is that your grandson would die before you do, especially by his own hand.

Anytime someone young dies, it's especially hard on the older members of the family, because it's so unexpected.

Once again, I was forced to re-examine my own life. I knew by now that I must've had a much bigger purpose, maybe writing this book and just getting my story out, who knows?!? I spent most of my time meditating, trying to prepare to take on this project. I had absolutely no clue how to go about trying to write a book, so I just wrote out all the main details in my life.

I focused mostly on the weird things that happened, and, as you can see, there was no shortage of these instances to write about. The more I examined and re-examined my life, writing and re-living each detail, I once again started to remember who I was before I died in that hospital.

And again, I began having even more vivid memories, always the same dapper guy, smoking away like a chimney. I've always had a fascination with gems and precious metals, since birth. I wondered if these memories had something to do with that.

Anywhere I went in Wheaton I knew I had already been there before. Every place I drove by, walked by, rode my bike by, whatever; I always pictured myself there in a far away time. I was absolutely sure of this. When I started to write this book, there was no doubt in my mind that I had lived before, on Earth, in a different body.

Unlike most people with advanced degrees, including doctorates, who write books, I felt that I had something that a lot of them didn't have: actual life and death experience. That is, I actually experienced and lived through what

I am talking about first-hand. What I know to be fact is not speculation, theories, or second-hand accounts of other peoples' stories. They are actual things that have happened to me.

I knew that I was most definitely reincarnated. I knew I died in that hospital, and was re-born as Jason. What I still didn't know was who I was in my past life and why I came back.

I started reading every book I could find on the topic and was amazed at the abundance of choices I had. I read so many of them I couldn't even tell you how many it was. What I can say is all of them were very interesting in their own ways. I especially like the ones where highly respected doctors were faced with reincarnation within their own lives, being forced to face the fact that a lot of the things that they learned, and taught others, were wrong. It can't be easy to build a whole career based upon misinformation and teach it to others within your field, only to realize that what you taught others wasn't true. Bravo, guys, for admitting you were wrong, and correcting that. You have greatly advanced our cause, to seek truth. I thank you very much.

These individuals also helped themselves a great deal by filling their own minds with the truth, further expanding their own consciousness as well. It made them re-think their lives too and wonder where they came from. It also made them go in an opposite direction with their lives and teachings. Once again, I thank them so much for having the courage to stand up and get these truths out to the public.

It's funny how we can help each other become enlightened by simply telling each other our stories. Once again, I think everyone should write an autobiography. I've always spoken of my experiences, and never swept them under the rug; that's not my style. I know for a fact that I have flipped many switches inside of other peoples' heads causing them to think or examine their own purposes while here on Earth. I know this because they tell me so.

Chapter 16

Evil Knows No Bounds

I now digress to the first anniversary of my brother's death. I knew it would be hard on Mom and Dad and I knew they'd need me for support. Little did I know that tragedy loomed near, yet again.

The previous night, I had the same disturbing feeling in my stomach that I knew so well. I just attributed it to nerves in anticipation of the next day. When I awoke in the morning my mom stopped by to say hi. We hung out for a while and then she left. About one minute had passed when she bolted back in through the door.

She had a totally shocked look on her face. She had just heard on the radio in her car that my good friend, Jennifer, had just been found dead only a few miles away from my apartment. I could not believe this was happening. What are the chances of her dying at the same time my brother did?!?

When I found out the morbid details I was furious. I was just over there about two weeks before when my friend Bubba and I installed her car stereo. Bubba and I went to the store and got the stereo. When we returned to the apartment, one of her friends, Pauline, was there. After we finished installing the stereo Bubba left, and it was just Jennifer, Pauline, and I.

We just hung out and talked for awhile, that's about it. Pauline appeared to be nice. Later that night I drove her home, not far from Jennifer's apartment. The next day I found out from Bubba that she was also her cleaning lady/caretaker. Jennifer was injured by an abusive ex-boyfriend and needed a caretaker. After hanging out with her once more, I came to the conclusion that she was really weird, downright nuts to be exact.

This was also around the time that Pauline told me she wanted to date me. I knew there was tension between them because Jen also told me that she had feelings for me. I barely even knew this weird girl. I never thought in a million years that this could happen.

One night in a violent premeditated rage, Pauline and two of her friends, broke, or were let into Jennifer's apartment building. Since Pauline worked for her, I imagine it was not too hard to get inside. I guess the details were that Pauline was so furious about being rejected that she hired those losers to rob and kill her.

As Jennifer lay sleeping in her bed, they crept in and attacked her. They ripped and twisted at her head, nearly decapitating her. When they heard her neck break, they thought she was dead. For their take in the murder they were to get some of her money and a whole bunch of pills, painkillers to be exact.

What I find most disturbing is that as they rifled through her stuff, Jennifer regained consciousness and begged for her life. The guy continued to beat and rip at her head until she was finally dead. Then they dumped her body in the bathtub like it was nothing.

I cannot comprehend how Pauline, this ignorant little girl, could have actually brainwashed these morons into such an act of sheer brutality. I believe she told them that Jennifer had a huge stash of cash and a large cache of pills, which she did not. She was very much low on cash, but did have a huge supply of pills in her safe. Pauline probably figured that by the time they saw that there wasn't much money, it would be too late. The deed would've already been done.

Wow, they must feel so unbelievably stupid for being manipulated by a little girl. Luckily, they have plenty of time to stew over that fact while they sit for life in an Illinois State prison. Too bad we're all paying for them to be in jail for many years.

Just when you think you're safe, "WHAM," you get killed right inside of your own home. If you think it can't happen to you too, think again. She lived in one of the safest places in the entire country, downtown Naperville.

The worst part about this whole tragedy is that Jennifer had a son. He was such a cute kid. I used to babysit him all of the time when they lived in Wheaton. I used to walk him to kindergarten, incidentally, the same exact kindergarten that I went to at Lincoln. They lived about five blocks west of the school.

I still laugh out loud to this day over his impression of the song "Breaking the Law." It is most hilarious to see a five-year-old boy stomp around with a dead serious look on his face, singing such a hardcore tune. Luckily, he's doing great.

He has served our country proudly in the Middle East, gotten a college education, and grown up to be a fine young man. His mother, as well as myself, are very proud of him!

About one year after her murder, Jennifer contacted me. It was about 11:00 P.M. and I had just turned off the television. My dog Puggles and I were just lying in the living room on the couch. As we lay there, I heard my name spoken in my ear in a very audible voice. It only said, "Jason, Jason."

I knew it was her immediately and even felt her breath in my ear. I absolutely froze. I was petrified. When I first heard her voice, I couldn't even turn my head to see her, I was so freaked out. Before I could even react, Puggles lept up from the couch and lunged towards my left ear, where the voice came from. It was clear that she too heard the voice and even saw Jennifer.

She backed up something, which was invisible to me, into the corner and just barked like a crazy animal. In the eight years since, I have yet to hear my dog growl like that, at anything. Thanks to Puggles, there was no way in hell that I had an auditory hallucination. Puggles disproved that without a doubt. Thanks Puggy!

Wow, it was so weird to hear Jen's voice again. Every hair on my entire body was standing straight up. I just lay there frozen for hours thinking about the visit I had just received. It did feel good to know that she was OK and was still watching over me. It just totally caught me off guard.

Jennifer's death seemed to be the catalyst for inspiring me to write this book. It seemed like something or someone was pushing me to write. It was a slow process, but finally I had a title. Next I designed a logo for the cover. Then I had my photos, layout design, and my drawings. It was necessary for me to coordinate each aspect myself, due to certain financial constraints.

CHAPTER 17

Discovery of One's Self

One of my most extraordinary experiences of all occurred when I was at Wheaton cemetery. While visiting friends and loved ones, my greatest discovery was revealed. I was sitting at my brother's grave. I moved over to my grandfather's grave, and just as it had occurred my whole life, I became fixated on his headstone. I just sat there staring at it and could not take my eyes off of it.

Once again I let everything go out of focus. I started to have tons of memories flood into me like a wave of consciousness. Everything in my present lifetime sort of blended with the memories I had from long ago. I started to remember names, faces, even dates.

I finally saw the view of both of my lifetimes in their entirety. All of the fragmented memories of my grandfather came together to form the life that I always seemed to remember. I saw everything leading up to, and including, myself dying in that hospital in New York.

It was like the fog just lifted right off of me. It was so amazing to finally see what happened to me leading up to my death. After all, it was the starting point for what I had always remembered. Until I had my epiphany that day, I just wasn't quite complete. Finally, my whole life as "Jason" made perfect sense.

All of the traits I exhibited since birth matched up perfectly with him, his career, his hobbies, everything. I finally understood what had happened. I died of cancer and heart complications in 1948 at a hospital in New York while on a business trip. I gasped my last breaths in a darkened hospital room trying to write my final wishes. Somehow, I was reborn as my own grandson.

I don't know why I came back, but I believe it was to watch over my youngest son, Dickie. He was only ten years old when I died. I found it totally unacceptable to leave my son without a father at such a young age. Little did he know, I have been closely watching over him for thirty-four years.

Well it was a huge relief finally understanding where I came from and why weird stuff always happens to me. It was also cool to finally know why I had all of those memories of Wheaton and Chicago, among many other places, from eighty years earlier. Oh, did I mention I was a published author ten times over in that lifetime too? Maybe that's what kept driving me to write this; maybe it's in me to write.

Chapter 18

Managing Fear

The wonderful thing is that anyone can achieve this self-discovery by meditation and or past life regression. Discovering who we were and what we did in our past lives can help us come to terms with why we act certain ways, or do certain things. It's especially useful with extricating your fears and or phobias.

People fear many things in this life, many different things actually. They all have one commonality: incidents in our past lives have helped to sculpt us into who we are and what we fear in this lifetime. Those characteristics also help us to avoid certain situations as a defense mechanism. Those fears, possibly a horrible death or a death of a loved one, are burned into our souls for a reason. That is where the term "past life trauma" comes from.

So, I guess in a way these phobias are somewhat useful; they make us think twice about doing certain things that might put us in harm's way. My mom has always been petrified to fly. She had a few close calls over the ocean in which her plane lost power and nose-dived. Someone suggested hypnosis and after a few short sessions she was totally cured. She frequently travels by plane now with no problems whatsoever.

Past-life therapy is very common nowadays and can be incredibly helpful. You have to understand, these memories can be very subtle. You have to pay very close attention to the nuances.

Speaking of fear, this brings me to another very important topic: medicine. These fears, or phobias, can manifest themselves in ways that we don't always notice. They can wreak havoc on our bodies and our minds by keeping us in a constant state of stress and/or anxiety without us even noticing. Symptoms can range from mild anxiety attacks to a debilitating nervous break down, not to mention a host of other issues.

Unfortunately, when people finally realize that they need some assistance, the first thing they do is run straight to their doctors and get put on dangerous drugs that aren't fully understood and can be deadly. They alter brain chemistry and can have horrible side effects.

If you are experiencing anxiety and it seems to come from inside, that is, with no obvious cause, I would highly recommend that you first try hypnosis and or past-life therapy before being put on dangerous pharmaceutical drugs. This is not to say that some drugs don't help some people; they do. It's just not necessary to give them out like candy to all of your patients. They are being given to millions of people that do not need them.

As I neared the completion of this book, I would endure another traumatic experience. I had an accident out at my house. I was on a ladder painting my kitchen. My puppy, Max, bumped the ladder that I was standing on, knocking me through a window. It was either land on him or go through the glass, so I chose the latter.

I nearly cut off my hand and was literally bleeding to death. I barely made it to the hospital before losing consciousness. The genius doctor in the emergency room dug around in my arm and came to the brilliant conclusion that I had narrowly missed my tendons. So he stitched me up and sent me home. I told him he was wrong and that I knew the tendons were severed.

I followed up with a hand surgeon and he gave me a similar diagnosis. He said that if I could move my thumb and fingers at all that they couldn't be severed. I said that he must be a really powerful, spiritually advanced being if he could just mystically see into my arm and tell me what I already knew from the start, that my tendons were totally severed.

I guess he wasn't so advanced after all because after months of my insisting that he actually open up my arm and look with his own eyes, he finally did. Now as I lie there being prepped for surgery, I briefly spoke to him and he assured me that I was probably going to wake up and he would be there telling me that none of my tendons were severed and everything was fine. He obviously was not taking part in reality, where I was hanging out.

CHAPTER 19

Watching From the Sideline

As they rolled me into the surgical suite, I was actually quite thrilled knowing that I was about to be unconscious. Consciousness has always been my favorite thing to think about. It's so amazing to me that we can leave our bodies and have no recollection of it. Then again, sometimes we do recall being unconscious and even may experience awareness while unconscious. Now, you're probably saying, how in the heck can you be aware while unconscious? It sounds like an oxymoron.

I can assure you that you will most certainly have awareness when your physical body is no longer living. I have always wondered why we can become unconscious and not remember, yet, during an out of body experience, or actual death, we are totally aware.

I would love to identify the reason that this occurs. I believe it has something to do with the severity of the detachment of the soul from the body. Possibly the level of trauma or even the manner of death may be factors.

It begs the question, "Where do 'we' go when we're unconscious?" We must go somewhere. I heard this explained most proficiently by an anesthesiologist who said, "How could I possibly put people under every day at work without wondering where they are going during the time that they are unconscious?" I'll bet he would be interested to know that not everyone is unconscious after he puts them under, and that some people retain their awareness while under anesthesia.

I applaud this anesthesiologist for embracing such an opinion and wished he had been in attendance at my surgery. As the gas mask hit my face, and I saw the I.V. drip, I started counting down from ten. By the time I hit five I found myself standing to the right of the operating table. I was clearly looking at the scene and could see my own physical body from a slightly elevated view from the distance of several feet.

I watched carefully as they joked and laughed about how much of a waste of time the surgery would be. The arrogant surgeon even had the nerve to say how he just wanted to get me out of his hair, and that I nagged him into the surgery in the first place. Once again, he reiterated the fact that he knew that the tendons weren't even going to be severed.

I just simply watched and listened, or observed, and was amazed at what I saw. When they opened up my arm, I could see all the parts and pieces. It looked really cool. It would've been absolutely disgusting to most people though. Ah, the look on Dr. Shan's face was priceless!

After all, he had just finished telling everyone in the room about how he knew for sure that the tendons weren't even going to be severed, and that the surgery was going to be a huge waste of time. Allow me to just say that, after a long series of medical errors by numerous so-called experts, my hand and arm are now permanently disfigured, disabled, and wracked with pain 24 hours a day. Thanks a lot, guys!

The only positive result to come from this whole fiasco was a sweet out-of-body experience. At least I had that, and the fuel I needed to spark more thoughts about where we go when we are unconscious. Well, I'd have to say that based on personal experience, I know that we go wherever our thoughts take us. We are all comprised of pure thought.

Usually when you slip into unconsciousness you do not remember anything after being anesthetized. This is obviously not always the case with me. I wonder if my ability to stay aware, despite being unconscious, has anything to do with my capability to remember my previous lives. I have a feeling that whatever this mechanism is that is keeping us from remembering each of these periods of lost time are one and the same. That is, I think that not being able to remember our past lives and not being able to remember being unconscious, are most definitely related.

Remember, the key to understanding why we do not remember these time periods is finding, and understanding this mechanism, or veil. Until we understand why our memories are blocked by this, we will only be held back in our evolution.

Chapter 20

The Illusion of Time and Movement

Another element blocking advancement is lack of information. I'd like to point out a few things that many people do not seem to know. One is that we are all immortal. I personally know this for a rock-solid fact, but some people find it hard to believe.

In order to fully understand time and immortality, you must first realize that time has little to do with immortality. Time is only a factor within the physical realm. It is nothing more than an Earthly measurement used to build guidelines. Its' primary function is to accommodate events such as the sun rising or setting or people being born or dying.

Just as inches, feet, yards, and miles don't apply in the afterlife, neither does time. Although consciousness appears to propel us forward, this is just the illusion that time projects. Look closely at this very moment and you'll see that we are in fact immortal right now.

We are living one continuous moment in which immortality is clearly visible. The only thing separating this moment, or breaking it into segments, is the sun rising and setting. This is what gives us the feeling that we are moving forward in time, a series of "days" that are strung together to seemingly create a "life."

We have to quit being tricked by this illusion. It traps us in a redundant cycle that we perpetuate daily, constantly doing nothing or going anywhere. It also tricks us into thinking that we all will eventually die. Not to say that our bodies will not, but remember, without our intelligent control, cars, like our physical shells, would never move. We simply get a new body once our current one is beyond repair.

Even when we reincarnate, the same moment still exists. It makes prefect sense that when I was in-between lives, twenty-six years blew by like it was just a few weeks.

This is because time only holds us back while we are occupying a physical body.

As I said earlier, these bodies are merely vehicles that our souls use in order to sustain life within this environment. Here is another thing to consider. While reading up on Quantum Physics, I came to realize some very interesting facts.

Every time we walk, talk, reach for something, etc, it appears that we are just moving as a solid mass. THIS IS NOT THE CASE! We are constantly disappearing and reappearing at the sub-atomic level. If you reach for something, you are not just moving your arm forward in a solid clump. The molecules that we are made of disappear and reappear billions of times in order for us to make that simple movement possible.

So your arm is actually disappearing and reappearing wherever you tell it to go. We take these simple movements for granted, but it is totally fascinating what is actually happening. Once again we have the physical body reacting to our single thought.

Obviously, for the brief period of time that we are invisible while making these movements, we don't even realize it. So, if we're constantly disappearing, where are we when we're not "here"? It kind of reminds me of being unconscious. Where do we go?

Well, it's simple. "We" don't go anywhere. It is not that "we" are disappearing, after all; it's simply our physical bodies. "We," the conscious observers, are always "here." That's why we don't notice that our bodies are constantly disappearing and reappearing.

Just to be clear, we are constantly disappearing and reappearing all of the time. We don't even notice because our souls are totally separate from our physical bodies.

Chapter 21

Understanding Dual Evolution

Now that you understand how we work, hopefully you can start to put everything together and see that we are all just spirits driving very fancy cars. When we separate the soul from the physical body, we can also see that reincarnation and evolution work perfectly together. Remember, life didn't evolve here on Earth overnight, and neither did our souls. It took a very long time. Reincarnation is also the bridge between spirituality and science.

Now consider this. As each species evolved, where that particular species ended up was solely in the hands, or claws, of said species. Choices that those animals made led them to instances that either helped, or hurt them. As each animal learned from the others' mistakes, they learned what to do and what not to do. This, in conjunction with the physical and environmental changes they were experiencing, allowed them to evolve.

Obviously, this took millions of years to happen. But as each species evolves, particularly humans, we become that much smarter. This increases the speed at which we evolve. So the more we evolve, the faster we evolve. The possibilities are truly endless. So lucky for us, we have plenty of "time" to learn and evolve. As long as we do not become complacent, and always seek the truth, we will evolve into much wiser beings.

In the fast-paced society of today, we must learn to slow down and live life in a more careful manner. I can tell you first-hand that you will not be happy if you're racing around one day and suddenly find yourself looking at your own dead body. You may not be as lucky as I was. It may be your time to go. Patience may be a lesson that you needed to learn in this particular lifetime, so be careful.

If you have children that are experiencing past-life memories, characteristics, psychic behavior, seeing spirits, or anything like that, please nurture their gifts and do not try to dismiss them. Denying these truths is ignorant, will only delay your child's advancement, and may even prove tragic for you, and them, later in life.

I also hope that you learned something from my life story. Or, at the very least, enjoyed reading about it. Remember, you never know whom you are really talking to out in the world. There are people on this Earth that are very powerful entities, who are thousands of years old, having lived many, many lifetimes.

One such entity has mastered his gifts and fine-tuned them into an art form, healing. He is an old man who not only sees and reads auras, but also he can correct them, or heal sick individuals. He is the one who taught me to do the same thing. When he enlightened me to the ways of the aura, I was changed forever. He awakened a healing power within me that we all have the capability to harness.

Well after I wrote and re-wrote this manuscript a bunch of times, it started to come together quite nicely. I'd like to take a second to point out that I had a lot of disbelievers telling me I was wasting my time and that I couldn't do it. Take note, I did it and it feels very rewarding to get my story out to be heard. We need more truth to be brought into the consciousness of humanity collectively.

Without truth in the world, our advancement will only be delayed further. We need the truth to discover what life is all about, or at least to better understand it. We'll probably never fully comprehend life in its totality, but we must at least try.

Now it seemed as though I had one more obstacle standing in my way. How would I find an ending to my book? Since it all actually happened to me, I sort of had to wait for something else to happen. This made me more than a little nervous. It was beyond frustrating to make it this far, only to be left without an ending. Stress was building and I was constantly agitated.

CHAPTER 22

Heavenly Jewels

It was around this time period that one day my mom and I got up and got breakfast at a local restaurant nearby. After breakfast we got into a big argument over this book, money, and bills. We screamed at each other and I bolted out of the house.

I jumped into my car and just sat in the driveway for a minute. The sun was blazing down on me through the windshield. Before I drove, I looked up at the sun and asked God to please show me a sign. I needed to know if I was on the right path or just wasting my life.

I asked God to strike me down at that very moment with a lightning bolt, a heart attack, anything, if I was not on the right path. I needed a sign desperately, and I believe that He knew that. At least my mom could get some money just in case the worst did happen.

At that exact moment, I felt a warm, loving presence beside me in the passenger seat. I couldn't see anyone, but I knew that they were there. I was compelled to drive the car out of the driveway and down the street. I had absolutely no destination in mind. In fact, I didn't even know if I was going to get struck down at any second.

I pulled out of my subdivision and proceeded east on Ogden Avenue. It was as if I wasn't even in control of the car. Some force was guiding me, or pulling me like a tractor beam. I was headed toward Naperville, but ended up at a resale shop near Fox Valley Mall.

I walked into the store and was drawn immediately to the jewelry case. This was totally out of character for me since I'd normally head straight to the back of the store where they kept the fish tanks and drums. Then I'd peruse the candle rack for some exotic scents. The jewelry case would be my very last stop on my way out.

As I looked into the case, one piece captured my attention immediately. It was a huge gold ring with a big blue stone. After waiting around forever for the employee to open the case for me, I reached right in and grabbed it.

It was very warm to the touch, almost hot. I noticed it was a large, perfectly centered Star Sapphire. It was a pretty heavy ring and it fit me perfectly.

When I looked inside of the ring, I was stunned to see that it said, "JASON 10K" inscribed inside. I couldn't believe it, I almost croaked. I showed it right to the girl who opened the case and, even crazier, it was only $3.99! Four dollars for a huge, solid gold ring with my name stamped right inside of it.

I knew I had just received a loud and clear sign from God that I was on the right path after all. To make this divine sign even sweeter, I asked the manager if anyone examines the jewelry before they put it out in the case. She told me that they have expert jewelers in the back who sort, identify, and price all of the jewelry that comes to the store.

"Oh, all the valuables don't even make it to the case. They go directly onto our website where people have to bid on them," she explained to me. I knew there was no way that such a large, clearly marked gold ring would escape the eyes of those shark jewelers.

I returned home astonished and told my mom what happened. I showed her the ring and she too couldn't believe what had happened. We just sat there and laughed, and everything was fine. After all, it was our argument that was the catalyst to ask for a sign in the first place.

Then I came to another realization, I not only just got a wonderful sign from the Heavens, I also had an ending for my book. How perfect is that?!? Numerous jewelers have examined the ring and determined that my name wasn't engraved in it; it was stamped there by the manufacturer. After months of searching, we found there is currently no jewelry manufacturer that uses my name as a hallmark.

I have seen thousands of pieces of silver, gold, and platinum jewelry, and never, ever have I seen a piece with my name inside of it. All of this was definitely no coincidence. You would have to be half-dead to dismiss this as luck, or a coincidence. I am convinced this was the sign for which I prayed.

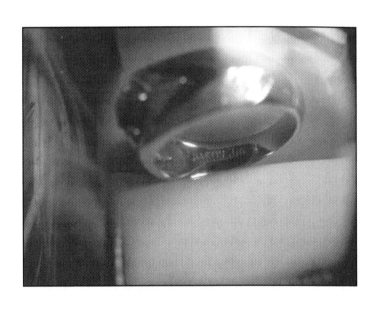

CHAPTER 23

Extricating Your Phobias

Let me emphasize this, I don't care what your religion is, what your paycheck says, how big your house is, or what kind of car you drive. I just want you to know that we are all spiritual beings who come to Earth to learn lessons. We need to learn these lessons in order to advance spiritually, or to become perfect. I'd like to also say that one of the most uninformed sayings I hear quite often is, "Hey, you only live once." I just laugh when I hear someone say that because I know for a fact that it couldn't be further from the truth.

It's amazing to me that everyone doesn't have the recall that I have. I even remember the phone numbers for every friend I ever had, going back twenty-five or more years. For some reason, I'm one of the lucky few who didn't have his memories blocked by the veil.

I cannot help thinking that we, as a Global Society, are on the verge of a huge shift in consciousness. I feel a new dawn of awakening emerging. There is just too much evidence to sweep it under the rug any longer.

People want real answers to their questions and are frustrated with the untruths that are being passed down through the generations. They want to know why we are here, who we are, and where we are going. I hope my story brings some level of comfort to anyone experiencing similar circumstances to my own. Rest assured, you are not alone.

We will soon find out amazing things about our lives here on Earth. Thanks to the process of Past Life Therapy, we can discover who we really are. Until we discover our true selves, we will only be strangers to our own minds, and prisoners to our own bodies.

The concept is quite simple. Your soul inhabits a physical body. Once that body dies, you go and get yourself a new one, just like a car, remember? There is one thing that worries me a bit though. Is there anything more frightening than a lifetime forgotten? Can you imagine going through all of life's experiences, only to forget it all? That's why we evolve so slowly; we only take with us things we fear. We need to do away with the fear in order to evolve faster.

Then we can control what we carry with us within our subconscious minds from lifetime to lifetime. I'd much rather have my talents or hobbies carry-over than my fears. We cannot break this cycle of fear until we understand this concept. Past life therapy should be done, if possible, by a certified hypnotherapist or hypnotist, who specializes in past life regression. I realize that not everyone has the finances for this, so another option is an at-home past life regression CD or DVD. It may take a few uses before you unlock any of your past life memories. If you don't notice anything, be patient, and remember, these memories can be very subtle. Do not get discouraged. Now that I know who I was, the world makes a lot more sense to me.

CHAPTER 24

A Little About Me

I had a really hard time believing that no one else remembered being born. I thought for sure someone did, at least one person. I have yet to meet anyone who remembers, but I'd love to hear from you if you do.

Another thing I noticed was the more I read about reincarnation, the more I realized how common it is to be re-born into your own bloodline. People in India accept this as a normal, daily occurrence. I would love to go there someday to visit. I have always been fascinated by the beautiful Taj Mahal. I wonder if I have ever lived there in a previous lifetime. I composed an in-depth report on it in Junior High.

As this book winds down, I want to make sure you understand this fully. I am the continuing consciousness of my own grandfather, Warren Piper. I was a world famous gemologist and owned gem-buying operations in Chicago, Amsterdam, Antwerp, London, and the Orient. I owned a high-end jewelry factory on Jeweler's Row in Chicago, where I hand-crafted and designed the finest platinum/diamond jewelry.

I made jewelry for Kings and Queens, movie stars, and Presidents. I was consulted by her Royal Highness, Queen Maria Braganza of Portugal, to re-assemble the Crown of the Andes, and actually owned the crown and many other jewelry components of the Braganza Crown Jewels.

I died in 1948 in a darkened room, but the light of God shone down on me and allowed me to re-enter the world as my own grandson, Jason. I came back not only to watch over my son, but also to deliver a message.

If you are the type of person that needs to see to believe, get ready for a long, long stay here on Earth. Life is much more than what meets the eye. It's more about trusting your heart and following it down a righteous path. The sooner we realize that true happiness can be achieved only by living many, many lifetimes, and learning from our mistakes, the sooner we can reside in our own versions of Heaven with our loved ones.

I believe the main point of these journeys are to graduate through them and learn from them, ultimately breaking the cycle of reincarnation via samsara, allowing us to reside in an environment free from pain and worry. Without these bodies holding us back, we are unstoppable. This also allows us to actually become the spiritual beings, or entities, that step in to help people in their times of need. Just the fact that we can intervene also allows others, still here on Earth, to see that there is, in fact, a higher power. We are ALL the higher power.

Our evolution is also very important to the Earthly assignments that we take on. We do have the power to intervene if we feel compelled to. If you think that you can't make a difference in the world, you are dead wrong (no pun intended.) Be the captain of your own ship, and do not let others dictate how you should live. God resides within all of us, and we must connect to our core, or soul, in order to tap into this divine light.

Just remember that everything you are seeing with your eyes is only a very minute fraction of what's really happening around you. Do not be narrow-minded.

Thinking in this way will only delay your own evolution and may even affect you negatively, especially when you come face to face with something that you didn't think was possible. And I implore you to READ people! Truth and knowledge really are power.

Thank you so much for taking the time out of your busy schedules to read my story. I really appreciate it, and I hope that it assisted you in your journey to self-discovery, or at the very least was an enjoyable read. I wish you all the best of lives. May you all find your truest loves, and embrace them throughout eternity.

SPECIAL THANKS...

Now I'd like to take the time to thank a few people: my mom, for being the best mom anywhere and always standing by me; my dad /son, for teaching me many things over the years and taking me all over the world, and, incidentally, for hanging on to all of my most precious trinkets that I handed down to him when I died; my brother, for trying so hard up until they day he died, being the best musician/ scholar I've yet to meet, and most importantly, for his ultimate sacrifice.

I'd like to thank my wonderful Mammy and Pappy; my Aunt Christmas; my step-grandfather, Dr. Theodore Boyd, PhD, for his love and for helping Dr. Jonas Salk bring the Polio vaccine into existence; Margie for filling in for Mammy temporarily and being a great step-grandmother;

Dawn and Patty for helping me edit this book over and over and for putting up with my craziness; Mr. D. for being the best teacher I have ever had; my other teachers for putting up with me over the years and filling me with knowledge; Jeff and Heather for their ultimate sacrifices and friendship; Jennifer for her friendship over the years, and of course, for her ultimate sacrifice; Mike and Floyd over at the Trading Post; Brent, Brian, Devon, Joe, Kyle, the other Brian, Melissa, and many more. Rest in peace my friends, may your spirits soar!

Finally, my biggest thanks goes to God and to my angels. Without them, none of this would have ever been possible. I wouldn't be here right now, and neither would this book.

"I once was my father's father, now I am my son's son."

j f m a m j **J A S O N** d
a e a p a u u u e c o e
n b r r y n l g p t v c

Additional information on this and other interesting topics may be found in the following books:

90 Minutes in Heaven by Don Piper, with Cecil Murphy (2004)

The Physics of Immortality by Frank J.Tipler (1994)

Children's Past Lives by Carol Bowman (1997)

Beyond the Ashes by Yonassan Gershom (1992)

Energy, Matter, and Form by Phil Allen (1975)

Journey of Awakening by Ram Dass (1982)

Phone Calls from the Dead by D. Scott Rogo and Raymond Bayless (1979)

Many Lives, Many Masters by Brian Weiss, MD (1988)

Reliving Past Lives: The Evidence Under Hypnosis by Helen Wambach, PhD. (1984)

Return from Tomorrow by George Ritchie, MD (1978)

Return from Heaven by Carol Bowman (2001)